Just a few poems

Just a few poems

By

Ernest N. Paquin

ISBN: 1-58721-587-X

1stBooks - rev. 6/20/00

About The Book

This is a collection of poems that can be carried off into many different directions but, all of them originated from the same place…good human thoughts. They were written using at least an ounce of every emotion known to me and me alone, they were written using insight from a possible (negative destiny), and they were written in appreciation of a basic simple plan (positive destiny). Let me explain;

> "I believe God's plan is so simple that the reason why mankind continues to work hard to confuse the idea, is due to the fact that it wasn't theirs…"
>
> &
>
> "Choices dictate destiny…or, keeps one from it."

Anyway, I hope you enjoy.

Ernest N. Paquin

TABLE OF CONTENTS

Introduction:

Poetry I believe can be the hardest form of literature to comprehend, so I've written in a way that can be understood not just by a specific class of readers but, by almost everyone. Now, here is a collection of poems written solely for those who are interested. They are simple, informative and at times witty but, they are all for good intensive purposes…in short, they mean well. Anyway, I hope you enjoy.

The Game

All around the world today
games are being played.
Some are big and some are small
some you just can't say.

There are also games you cannot see
these are kept well hidden.
Not everyone shall play these games
to most they are forbidden.

There is one game that does request
that all contribute their part.
But if one jumps from side to side,
It will rip their soul apart.

No need to worry, no need to fright
but make these words understood.
“If one chooses to be led astray
maybe it's best that he should.”

It’s wise to use caution in joining a belief
because you won’t know what’s instore.
Like a boat sailing away at sea
you may never return to shore.
They shall never reveal unto thee
whom they truly serve.
They are bound however to ask you once,
“what do you think you deserve?”

If this happens, do not worry,
remember it's just a game.
But never ignore the fact of the matter
the rules shall remain the same.

Now if you want out convince yourself,
“they cannot make me stay.”
This is true believe it or not
so consider this thought today.

You'll be alright I know it
so take care of yourself and don't blow it.

Forget all about, what raises a doubt
and get on with your life as you know it.

Faces

Evil is amongst us
this is certainly true.
Beware of this little devil
for he might just come in two's.

One comes with a smile
the other with a frown.
You can't have one without the other
they help the world go round.

Many people believe in this
I for one do not.
I believe in good no less
this one should be taught.

It very seldom is because
it takes so long to deliver.
Many become the taker
very few become the giver.

Now, the one that has the smile
shall offer you many things.
All you have to do for him
is let him pull your strings.
The one that has the frown
shall prey upon compassion.
Give an inch, he'll take a mile
tricky but that's his fashion.

Now you know he has at least two faces,
believe me this is true.
Be prepared for multiple attacks,
nothing less than two.

The EYE

Everywhere you look today
something passed you by.
It was meant to be that way
unless you caught the EYE.

It shall be evasive towards the few,
it cannot lead astray.
But the many that choose to look for it,
play into dismay.

It'll trap you in a corner
of a little tiny house.
It'll play a deadly game with you
just like cat and mouse.

It shall put you through a series of tests
in hopes that you shall fail.
Just when you think you've succeeded at this
It'll have you chasing your tail.

It does not care if it wins or not
so long as it holds you steady.
It can decide if you live or die
but won't say until it is ready.
The best thing I can tell you is
try and look straight ahead.
Don't get involved with what you don't know,
observe others who've caught the Eye instead.

They shall wear a look upon their face
that will show you what I mean.
Never ask what has happened to them
they might just start to scream.

"Mind your own business!!," they also will add
for the sake of observing you'll wish that you had.
They won't be the same from whom you once knew
and there shall be many and not just a few.

I will never stop looking for victims
it craves and longs for this.

It shall patiently cater to tempted souls,
with weaknesses they cannot resist.

Always remember just what I've said,
and I pray it truly sinks in,
It shall always be in search of those,
little people called children.

SECRETS

Secrecy is a big part of the game,
keeping it will assure you of fame.
The hard thing about it is earning ones trust
and as the saying goes, this is a must.

There are two types, the bad and the good
who are always at constant battle.
If you honor one, you can't the other
both are in fear you'll tattle.

The bad approach with a counterfeit smile,
I mean with an infamous grin.
The good ones however shall smile as well
with a glow right above their chin.

Now the good secrets might sound like the bad
if you didn't choose these you'll wish that you had.
I'm not gonna explain in case bad should hear
but listen with your conscience and they shall appear.

I have just revealed two different choices
but like many others you'll hear many voices.
Don't just go with what I have to say
listen for yourself they'll appear everyday.
I would just like to add, be cautious in choosing
for many heard wrong and ended up losing.
Just use your conscience tapped into your heart
if you listen without it, it'll tear you apart.

The (H)

If you have a problem
try not to submit
put an (H) on your chest
and handle it.

The (H) represents
the hold that you need
keeping problems suppressed
or else others will feed.

They shall poke fun
and add to the fire,
so ignore all of those
who crave that desire.

They'll push all your buttons
down to the very last one.
adding weight to your problem
that'll feel like a ton.

So don't tell them nothing
cause' they already know
and by offering their cures
is truly just for show.
So swallow your pride just like a man
and put it behind you as fast as you can.
Time heals all, it's a God-given fact
so just hold on tight and try not to react.

I am telling you this
cause' I've been through a lot
and when I reacted
I always got caught.

I'll tell you something else
in hopes it'll sink in
keep an eye on your patience
so it doesn't wear thin

Now remember the beginning of the poem I just wrote
and I'll end all of this on a serious note,

A problem you may have shall sting quite a bit
so put an (H) on your chest and handle it.

HIS TARGET

The target he seeks is our youth
It’s not a myth but the absolute truth.
It's rather easy you must admit,
he catches them all before they gain wit.

He appears to miss some,
but doesn't give up the chase
he'll snag them in a different way,
quicker without haste.

He shall long to do so,
and never ever stop
He's not content with what he has,
it's what he hasn't got.

I can't tell you how to avoid him,
but I can give you a clue.
Now listen to what I'm saying,
because all of this is true.

He doesn't care what beliefs you share,
he'll take what he can get.
He does however look for those,
that never show regret.
When he sees that you’re a standout,
you'd better watch your back.
You'll never see him coming,
you're his favorite kind to attack.

He'll shower you with gifts,
for things that you've achieved
You might think you earned them,
but you've truly been deceived.

And once you've accepted these gifts of deceit,
you can't just give them back.
But you can however avoid this catch,
and this sort of attack.

Just remember all that I've said
And I pray it makes solid sense.

But look with your conscience and you shall be find,

that it's your best form of defense.

MONEY

The name of the game is making money
it's the most common way to behave.
All there is to it, is to find ones weakness
and feed them what they crave.

Some people will literally sell their soul
to get the ALL-MIGHTY dollar.
It's a work of art in tearing one apart,
by making them stand up and hollar.

"More, more," is what they'll say
"Not tomorrow, I need it today,
I can't go without it, please give it to me."
One must submit in order to receive.

They will act like puppets I also might add,
begging like they do, makes others mad.
It's not really them that appear before you
but the craving that they have, this much is true.

Many don't care they just like the money
they'll crawl over other bees to get to the honey.
"Study the past," one president said,
after that warning, he ended up dead.
What I'm really trying to say
is don't make money the same way.
Try and find an honest route
that's what success is all about.

LUCK

If one was to find something they lost
Only then would they consider it luck.
But if they looked hard they would realize fast
it wasn't really gone it was stuck.

It was caught in a place that has no name
and the world can't exist without it.
It has a purpose that can be explained
so I'll try and tell you about it.

Stand straight up and hold something in your hand
relax and let it fall to the ground.
If you look with both eyes and watch where it lands
you'll see how easy it was found.

Now close both your eyes and try it again
you'll begin to see what I mean.
Open them now and look towards the ground
whatever you've dropped can't be seen.

I might be second or two or three
but it took you some time to find it.
It's like reading a book, if you know how to look
through each sentence and behind it.
I guess what I'm saying with all this delaying
is try and look with more than your eyes.
If you just go with these, you might get deceived
and be in for a total surprise.

WARNINGS

Warnings are messages given unto thee
to guide oneself to their destiny.
If you fail to listen, you just might be dense
if you choose to adhere, you use common sense.

I'm not saying this to put anyone down
I'm trying to make you understand.
I know it's not easy to escape temptation
it's like running uphill in the sand.

You think you can do it all by yourself
like reaching for cookies placed high on a shelf.
From where your standing it doesn't look very far
but once you've reached them, there is nothing in the jar.

I know this poem sounds like a riddle
it was meant to be that way,
but if your dealing with temptation
turn away from it today.

Now what I’ve written is a simple attempt
to help you think much better.
Ignore what others may have to say,
because to them this is only a letter.

PO-LIE-TICS

Many players in this game
understand the Po-lie-ti-cal step.
They have many rules that must be observed
and secrets that have to be kept.

No disrespect to some in the least
I'm only stating a fact.
Come elections they begin to lash out
with illiberal and back-stabbing tact.

The people they shall serve, take notice of this
and are really left with no choice.
They're compelled to elect one or the other
so they choose the one with the voice.

It doesn't make sense to spare no expense
with the costs once they are in there.
Because they can't do too much, with the inobvious crutch
from their past that appears from nowhere.

Some players don't care, they just want the juice
to help all their friends who have ends that are loose.
It's the same old game, term in term out,
and that's what the Po-lie-ti-cal step is about.

NO DIFFERENCE

I will tell you the difference
between dealer and addict
and also the difference
between radical and fanatic.

A dealer is he who supplies the addict
with whatever it is he may crave.
A radical is he who pushes the fanatic
just how he wants him to behave.

But someone believes you need all of these
in order for this world to make money.
It kind of makes sense to anyone who's dense
you need something that stings to make honey.

Protect our investments they'll tell everyone
regardless of what the cost.
But if you help them achieve with what they believe
any hope for the future is lost.

So do the world a favor and to yourself
go to the library, grab a book off of the shelf.
Read all that there is and try to adhere
and the rules to the game shall become very clear.
Many of you know exactly what I'm saying
the four that I mentioned always end up betraying
Not just each other but you and me too,
a very good point that's undeniably true.

(this is in favor of the Drug free America campaign…
(also for the Peace on earth campaign…)

ANTI-

Everyone in the world today
happen to be anti-something.
Wouldn't it be nice just for a change,
for all to be anti-nothing.

There is anti-white, anti-black
yellow, brown and red.
It's truly hopeless to choose one of these
because racism all in your head.

I have a solution to this whole problem
if anyone cares to hear this.
Start with a test of faith no less
then focus on a common interest.

Then weed out the problems amongst each other
by removing every ounce of confusion.
Then start up again by teaching our youth,
and there will lie the solution.

This is all for the good, so I can't say too much
just in case bad should hear.
But consider this thought, that I've modestly taught
and the anti- shall disappear.

MR. CORRUPT

Mr. Corrupt works on a daily basis
he disguises himself with many different faces.
Then you have officers that chase after him
who is very hard to catch at times aided from within.

I'm not putting down those that wear a shield
I'm only stating a fact because this stuff is real.
I do however have a request
all who wear one should undergo a test.

I do not doubt their oath,
or the training they took.
I do suggest that this be done
to snag the brightest of crooks.

You know the one, he slips through the cracks
and with a hidden knife stabs others in their backs.
He does all of this to get to the top
pretty vindictive for one crooked cop.

He plans all of this from the very beginnning
and always get pinched and never ends up winning.
Just like the others he'll eventually get caught
and so ended the lesson deservedly taught.
But soon there will be others that'll get hip to this
and slip through other cracks that already exist.
So don't get sucked in by the corruption you see
just do your own thing and let life get rid of thee.

The Law

The law might be for thinkers
to find all little cracks.
They will slither through them like a snake
and avoid all the little traps.

It all begins with a single act
and branches just like a tree.
They could kill a dozen people or more
and still remain scott free.

They no longer have a conscience
and don't worry about being caught.
They withhold this wisdom from all the others
by not showing them how they were taught.

They can only hint their rule to this world
“nothing in life shall be free,
you must think hard and connive alot
in order for one to achieve.”

Thou must not copy anyone else
cause' your angle alone is the test.
Once you've succeeded all by yourself,
he will consider you one of the best.
He will use you in his future plans
knowing you will not fail.
But you should be cautious of feeling welcome
you will end up chasing your tail.

You won't rightly know whom you will serve
that first particular task.
But when it's all over you'll soon find out
cause' then he'll remove his mask.

You will not like what's behind the mask
and you can forget about ever getting out.
Once you've been tricked into joining his clique
Its over, and that's what it's about.

Now the only way to avoid this catch,
along with a certain fate.

Is don't do the crime, and you won't do the time
observe others who have taken the bait.

INHERITORS

Now I know why it remains a secret
certain people know just how to keep it.
They're the ones who shall inherit the earth
they've known all about this since mans first birth.

Their main concern is to get rid of bad
I have to admit, for this I am glad.
But evil will counterfeit this master plan
and will try and conquer the goodness of man.

It's all very clear and right in front of you
I can't rightly say in case evil hears too.
The best I can hint is," don't be lead astray,
use your conscience and pay attention today."

What I can say in hopes you understand
is to learn the right language as fast as you can.
Use it in a good sense and never in vain
many have taken that route, and all of them were slain.

I'm only going to comment, maybe just a little
just in case evil is reading this riddle.
But I hope for mans sake you truly choose good
this much I pray becomes understood.

THREE TINES, NOT TWO

All through life many are faced
with choices that are new.
But if they look at them like fork
they'll see three tines instead of two.

What I'm trying to say is the average fork does
just because it's supposed to.
The dinner fork has four, the salad fork has three
and the pickle fork has only two.

They all have a purpose and all are a choice,
now listen to this riddle
When your unsure and there is no other voice
choose the one in the middle.

You can't go wrong and no one can laugh
just because you've chosen this path.
You might gain praise or you might hear a boo
but you certainly picked right seeing three tines,

and not two.

(I encourage all young kids to remain nuetral…)

PURGATORY

Many men have their own story
of this place they call purgatory.
I myself have my own notion
to settle this matter that causes commotion.

The lifetime one lives is constantly viewed
by two different Idealists.
Obstacles are placed in front of ones face
by both who know how to conceal this.

They shall offer to control ones own fate
by giving them a choice whom to serve.
But once he chooses, he sometimes loses
and reluctantly gets what he deserves.

He then asks "Why?" after he cries
"Why did this happen to me?"
He then hears a voice, "It's because of your choice,
that caused this harm to come upon thee."

"I don't understand I'm only a man
I thought I was doing good."
"That's the point that had to be made
anything can be misunderstood.
Once again he heard the voice
that gave him a chance to repent his choice.
"You shall be punished for the wrong that you've done
take heed to this lesson and teach to everyone."

"One day you shall die and answer to me
teach many others and I shall forgive thee.
Begin with your son and pass it along
do what is right and you shall fix what is wrong."

Once again, I'm giving you a riddle
but the lifetime you live lies right in the middle.
You shall be judged pending your life story
a decision shall be reached, then no more purgatory.

FAME

Few achieve this and when they do
they tend to abuse it cause' they don't think it through
How? I'm asking, can they do this to fans
ruin their own image and future plans.

They must serve a purpose to he who is bad
so when they do fall I am certainly glad.
They lose their future of glitter and gleam
and are no longer a spark in the eyes of a teen.

It doesn't stop with them for all that they did
it effects everyone especially some kid.
It takes only one to create this big wave
and just for a little while will others behave.

It'll soon blow over and rise up again
it's not very hard, they know right where to begin.
Where the others left off is where they'll start
and it won't be long before they too fall apart.

There you have it, the price some will pay
just for leading their own life astray.
It does a lot of damage and causes great pain
to the many who admire those that reach fame.

RULES

Rules are things that govern a state
simply put, they legislate.
At times they favor those that are cruel
and if you think about it, they're evil's favorite tools.

He uses these rules to protect all his friends
causing most if not all to bend.
Just far enough to open a crack
so the evil in men know where to attack.

They weaken the structure of the initial intent
causing them to fold up as easy as a tent.
Then many loopholes shall begin to appear
for the uncaught criminal to further his career.

He climbs up the ladder quick as whip
laughing at others thinking he's hip.
But what he didn't see that was hidden from thee
was a small bit of knowledge that was not on the tree.

It's just a little secret that good always kept
hidden from those that followed this step.
It shall remain hidden until such a time
shortening the ladder to this hideous climb.
Try and remember all that I've said
and bury all this in the back of your head.
"All through life you will hear of many fools,
who will try to succeed by abusing the rules.

DEMONS

They are the devils hand-picked doers,
that venture forth and serve thee.
They acquire good things and twist them around
that contribute to his destiny.

But what they don't know, because it doesn't show
is the trust he doesn't give to any.
He makes them believe, the trust he gives thee
is bountiful, infinite and plenty.

So when it all ends and truth finally comes out
they'll flee from the realm they are serving.
But little do they know, cause' it'll violently show
the wrath that punishes the deserving.

They'll try to refute and repent their sins
and the good they twisted for him.
then all shall cry and begin their screamin'
due to the fact at one time they were demons.

THE SECRET OF LOVE

Love is a word that is used to adore
Correctly expressed it means amour.
It's a bond one shares with another,
similar to that between a father and mother.

They care for each other in the highest degree
shaping and planning a joint destiny.
If he takes the wrong path, she puts him on track
if she walks away, he tries to get her back.

As they grow older, their bond grows stronger
years go by fast and the love lasts much longer.
Until one departs leaving the other behind,
with memories to cherish and thoughts of all kind.

The love is always there, no doubt about it
it's hard to go on living without it.
For the other I mean, who lost their best friend
who keeps love immense even after the end.

It takes a while for the crying to stop
but the love that they shared simply does not.
The bond shall mature in Heaven above,
the original meaning behind the secret of love.

CHECKMATE

All through life you will see several moves
made by nature that leaves many grooves.
The point to it all is to open your eyes
as to what's taking place, so you won't be surprised.

If you fail to witness these certain acts,
your enemy or foe will start their attack.
By confusing your ways and rushing your fate,
limiting your freedom and forcing checkmate.

They shall start by toying with you just a little
unfolding to you one of their riddles.
Then just when you think you have it all figured out
nature moves again, showing another route.

Once again it shall force you to think
and it might push your mind up over the brink.
So try not to ponder on your next move
go with your instincts, you might find the groove.

Once in a lifetime throughout this war
one shall find a route to even the score.
Then his groove, will place him back in the middle
fully prepared for an upcoming riddle.
That will again challenge his faith and health
assuring him of fame or take all his wealth.
I guess what I'm saying before it's too late
is find the right groove and avoid checkmate.

POEM # 23

I am writing about an unbelievable place
many don't think exists.
It manifested from the origin of man
and will enter this world from the abyss.

It has no definite color
but uses a shade from them all.
It has no size nonetheless
but is wide and rather tall.

It has no eyes but can truly see
and watches over all of thee.
It has no ears, but can also hear
the sounds of the world that do not appear.

I guess what I'm saying is everyone's being watched
(24-7) around the clock.
If you have a conscience, you'll listen to me
if you don't have one, I feel sorry for thee.

So watch what you do and try not to get snagged
if you follow the wrong path your bound to get bagged
Just use your head and you won't be hurt
cause' you're completely useless 6 feet in the dirt.

SSHHHH...

Everyone's been asked, "You want to hear a secret?"
Some answered yes and knew just how to keep it.
Some of them couldn't, unlike those who had
the question I pose, "Was it good, or was it bad?"

The secret I mean, was it used for the good
or used for the bad and simply misunderstood.
It's just another tradeoff that many will take
before they find out it was truly a mistake.

I guess what I'm saying, is it's not the way to go
if you don't want to hear it just simply say no!
Because evil secrets will come to the surface
and no doubt succeed in their original purpose.

Believe me I know, it's hard to keep a secret
once you find out what it's about.
So just turn your head, don't hear what was said
and don't get involved with a doubt.

THE WOOL BITERS

At times they may catch you by total surprise
pulling the wool up over your eyes.
I guess what they did was simply deceive
an intolerable act some wouldn't even conceive.

Of doing to someone who appears to be lost
pillaging them with no added cost.
Make no mistake they hide from the law
and are just like vampires, vulgar and raw.

They attack from all angles in the brightest of ways
casting many lures to hook all their prey.
They use the wool to make things more dark
they then sink their teeth and always leave a mark.

They shall drink until their bellies get full
or until light returns getting rid of the wool.
A part of your life has been taken from you
and can never be returned, this much is true.

The CLIQUE

They have many eyes, they have many ears
they see and listen to all that appears.
Their main objective is to find who is different
then seek and destroy who fear their commitment.

To he of course, who leads their pack
telling them who, when and where to attack.
He will not physically use his own hands
he will however, issue commands.

Without any questions they shall be carried out
cautious of a few that might carry a doubt.
But just in case a spy gets inside
he shall prove to him there is nowhere to hide.

They will never reveal the oath that they took
to those who can't practice the rules from the book
That have been handed down from father to son
and shall be carried out until the end has begun

There is a strange twist to the poem I just wrote
and I end all of it on a serious note.
He that they serve is simply misunderstood
because the knowledge he has, he stole from the good.

WHY AM I HERE?

What is going on, why am I here?
you've known all along I'd be living in fear.
Not of my shadow, nor of my fate.
but the world that surrounds me that brings forth my hate.

You put me on earth as part of your plan,
with very little guidance and knowledge at hand.
You gave me a conscience and a heart as well,
that I pray I've used wisely to deliver me from hell.

You may be offended but I really have to ask,
what is the point, and what is thy task?
Sometimes I wonder if I have to choose a side,
and reveal a secret I have locked up inside.

But what if I don't choose and stay in the middle
by suppressing this secret leaving everything a riddle.
About a game being played that's perfectly clear,
and keeps me wondering why am I here?

I need not ask who is to blame,
for the arrogance involved in this terrible game.
I shall patiently wait for your point to be made
and for the goodness in man to come forward and save.
All those who strayed from the true beat and path,
who've been tempted by Evil, who now sits back and laughs.
I guess I shall see because you've always been near,
and my question shall be answered, "Why am I here?"

DE JA VU

It's what good or evil may have instore,
from the illusion of having done it before.
It's a weird feeling I also might add
you wonder if it's good or if it's bad.

Now here's an idea that does come to mind
what if the illusion is from another time?
From a long time ago in the very beginning
to remind you again that you keep on sinning.

Or maybe it's telling you you're on the right path
immune to disease and the well deserving wrath.
That's been cast upon man for the wrong he has done
to a father, mother, daughter, and son.

When this occurs, stop and check out
what the life that your living is truly about.
If you acknowledge the fact, its dishonest or true
remember you've been warned by the illusion of
DE JA VU.

THE MASK

Dearly beloved we are gathered here today
to lead yet another sad life astray.
Make him older, a tad bit bolder,
and he will no doubt walk this way.

we shall tempt him in doing whatever we want
that's never and easy task.
The risk at stake and the energy it'll take
to get him to wear the mask.

The mask is something kept in his pocket
when all the other remedies fail.
He'll reach deep inside and place it over his eyes
and it shall slowly start to unveil.

Everything he wanted but couldn't have before
that acts like a key to a well-hidden door.
That many have been welcomed to venture on through
who reached in their pockets, and put on the mask too.

Part 2

Well just like a dream it didn't last very long
cause' when he took it off, all he wanted was gone.
"What just happened?" is what he will ask
it all went away when he took off the mask.

That's what happens when you're down on your luck
you reach in your pocket and your hand gets stuck.
You pull out your hand and you confusingly ask,
"where in the hell did I get this mask?"

I'll give you a hint, you're pretty close to it
I'll give you another, if you have it, don't use it.
Wear it I mean, what else would I say?
I kid you not, it will lead you astray.

You'll reach this stage in your very own life
troubled with grief, dismay and strife.
"What's this in my pocket?" is what you will ask,
all the wrong things confined to a mask.

The next two poems are dedicated to my children (my little fellas). Nate short for Nathaniel and Eric. Nate, the youngest of the two, at times feels left out due to the fact that his older brother who has a handicap, appears as if he's shown more patience towards. There are many single fathers like myself or married even, that have somehow shared everything he has equally with his children. Also, he must warn them of the many types of evils that shall never stop coming after them. It truly is a difficult job being a father with the questions that might arise at any given moment, and the challenges that seem to constantly burden him. But it's an adventure that any true father wouldn't even think about walking away from…being a parent in this world is our job, not God's…

50/50

There was a little boy
his name was Nate.
He wasn't very old
he just turned eight.

He felt left out
because he was smaller.
Got mad at his brother
because he was taller.

"Why can't I be
as big as Eric, Dad?"
I assured him he would be
for this he seemed glad.

"But it will take a little while
so don't be in a hurry.
If you grow up too fast
your Daddy will worry."

"In the meantime
you stay my little fella."
We went and got some ice cream
his favorite was vanilla.
What I'm truly trying to say is,
my two boys are just a kick.
Being Daddy is just part of it
50/50, now that's the trick.

The Secret

The devil came to town one day
but forgot his trinkets at home.
So he reached in his pocket
pulled out some coins,
and bought everything up on his own.

He didn't buy fair
he most certainly cheated.
But when one took the bait
the rest had conceded.

Except for one man
who saw through this ploy.
and he didn't have much,
except for one little boy.

As stubborn as he was
the man wouldn’t give in.
Because he knew if he did

the devil would win.

He fought long and hard
but the devil's deed was done.
He died because of this
for the sake of his son.
All that was witnessed
by that one little boy.
Enraged him enough
to challenge this ploy.

So he stepped to the devil
escorted by pride.
And chastised him verbally,
Ignoring his size.

After hearing these words
that the little boy posed.
A grin had appeared from
beneath the devils nose.

"Such harsh little words

from a small little boy
for this the test of faith
I shall truly enjoy."

"I will not lash out
at this precise time.
Instead, I'll wait generations
to get what is mine."

"I will not tell you when
it shall be a surprise.
But, by looking at you,
I shall remember those eyes."

"I hope that you do,"
the little boy said,
as he looked down at his father
he knew who was dead.

"I shall remember as well,
and that look in your eyes,
and when we do meet again

it shall be you that's surprised."

Upon hearing these words
the devil tipped his hat.
He smiled of course
And was about to turn his back, when…

The boy took after him
quick as a whip.
But he wasn't that fast
because of his hip.

He walked with a limp
for the whole world to see.
The devil took notice
and showed no sympathy.
He then told the child
"You have quite a task,
I shall savor the future,
when it arrives from our past.

Now how could this boy

at the tender age of six,
beat the devil himself
with only the aide of a stick.

He thought long and hard
until finally it clicked.
They boy knew at that moment
how the devil could be licked.

He kept it a secret all to himself
he then turned and walked away.
Like a shiny penny in his pocket
he would save it for a rainy day.

Finally the devil left the town
and would return another day.
And the townsfolk who sold out to him
Gave him thanks and praise.

The town must become one-sided
the devil had demanded on that.
But that one little boy who kept a secret

would wait until he came back.

PART 2

It wasn't for some time
when the devil had returned
and much to his disliking,
only one refused to learn.

It just so happened to be
a little boy who was six.
But from what the devil could recall,
he used to walk with a stick.

Nonetheless, no need to worry,
the devil would handle this problem.
So he stepped to the boy and rigidly asked,
"Why is it that you are not like them?"

The boy replied,"I was told long ago
exactly what had happened to them.
I am just fine so leave me alone
they are the ones with the problem."

"I am only a boy and not yet a man.
They are all wrong says the law of the land.
I can see this for I am not blind.
Now be on your way, if you would be so kind.

Without further ado
the devil stepped back.
He felt truly unsure
of this sort of attack.

He didn't really care
so he just walked away.
For this little boy, he thought,
was only a stray.

Ho posed no threat.

not at this time.
So the devil went on
to serve those in line.

"Wait just a minute, "
the little boy said.
"I have fooled thee
and your reign is now dead."

The devil looked back
and stared at the kid
and with a mean look said,
"I don't think you did."

" For I am the one
who shall always reign high.
You are merely a boy
one year more than five."

"Just answer me this,
where is thy cane?
That you needed the aide of

when your father was slain."

"That is the trick
that's been played upon thee,
for that was some other
because it sure wasn't me.

"What do you mean
you spunky little brat?!"
The devil demanded
as he took off his hat.

"Just what I said,"
the little boy mentioned.
"Your reign is now dead,"
and that got his attention.

The devil demanded,
"Explain what you're saying,
I am getting quite peaved

with all this delaying."

"I can't explain it
but maybe he can,"
as he pointed to the porch
graciously with his hand.

Out of a chair
arose a man who was lame,
who had to carry himself
with the aide of cane.

As he limped off the porch,
and sat down by the boy.
The devil assumed
it was some kind of ploy.

It got him to think
about what he had done
a long time ago
to the father of this son.

Shocked he added,
"I have been fooled
you are right about that,
but explain this to me,"
as he put on his hat.

"If the key to this secret
lies in the mind of a child
reveal it to me,
and I shall make it worth while."

"It is faithfully unwise
for me to truly say
you're very much aware of this
now please, go on your way."

The devil put on his hat and left
knowing his reign was done.
Then the boy looked at his dad
once they knew that they had won.

Smiles covered both their faces

and the townsfolk were mad at this.
A boy and his dad had beaten the devil
without even raising a fist.

Now, I'm not gonna say just how they did it
that would be telling the secret.
But I'll give you a hint if you value your soul,
buy a penny's worth of insight and keep it.

These next two poems belong to my personal beliefs. I'm not trying to come across in an off beat way or provoke chaos but, I am trying to warn you of what might come about in the future. Many rich and powerful men have read one of the many Bibles out there with all of them basically agreeing on the same thing. Now I believe that if these men have taken it "word for word," then it's possible that they will hold Good men to it by swearing to all that is written in it. Simply put, if it began with God placing everything into mankind's hands, is it safe to say that God will place wrath there too?...or will it be man's wrath?

" Good men may have wrote the Bible but, Evil men swear by it..."

THOU SHALL BE DONE

I'll tell you a story about a master plan
that came from visions given unto man.
It might open the eyes of those who are reading
and could alter the views of those non-believing.

In the word, that God has (offered) unto thee
to shape and form the worlds destiny.
Once you've searched and you yourself found it
your eyes shall open to all that surrounds it.

You'll see beauty, peace and the key to the door
that shall lead you back to the way it was before.
Prior to all the evil that's been done
to a father, mother, daughter and son.

Faith will guide you throughout this life
believe in this tool and it will steer you from strife.
Sit back and observe all that's being done
and patiently wait for the arrival of God's kingdom.

Oh it's going to happen, just give it some time.
Ignore those who say, " you're out of your mind."
It's all been written since man's first birth
as it is in Heaven, it shall be on earth.

MY INTENTION

Finally I'm writing you one last poem
about a nice guy, maybe you know him.
He is cursed with a very big heart and conscience,
and the way he thinks might sound like nonsense.

What he's trying to do is make our youth aware
of a terrible game that's played everywhere.
He's not doing this for profit or fame
he's trying to warn many, " don't partake in this game."

So try not to think he's out of his mind,
he's trying to warn who's worthy of mankind.
Of the pain he endured through the course of this game
so others can avoid it and not end up ashamed.

Thou should respect yourself and your foes.
I know it's not easy because God only knows.
The fate one deserves when their own life is done,
and all that goes on shall end under the sun.

I really can't help that it sounds like a riddle
and just like the others, it lies right in the middle.
The point I'm making, what else can it be?
by warning our youth not to do unto thee. (remain neutral)

****

The poems here written within are dedicated to our future...God love ya.

Ernest Norman Paquin

P.S. All you young people out there are allowed to remain neutral....

About the author

My name is Ernest Norman Paquin and I have two boys ages 8 and 9. I have been a correctional officer for over 10 years and have endured as much enduring it took to realize that; "If I had failed to change my ways while in my youth, I could have very well ended up in prison…on the other side." So, I've come to the conclusion that "it's much easier to go to jail than it is to stay out", and what I have to offer now are even simpler warnings other than the poems you just read;

> " Don't think for a moment that you have to learn or believe what you were taught in school, you don't…however, if you wish to succeed legally in this world, then it's wise to remember everything…"

&

> " Once your conscience leaves you in this world, you become fair game…"

&

" It's unfair to corrupt God with a color…even more so man's beliefs."

www.ingramcontent.com/pod-product-compliance
Ingram Content Group UK Ltd.
Pitfield, Milton Keynes, MK11 3LW, UK
UKHW040017200726
13854UKWH00001B/251

9 781587 215872